Our Physical World

Motion

by Rebecca Olien

Consultant:
Philip W. Hammer, PhD
Vice President, The Franklin Center
The Franklin Institute
Philadelphia, Pennsylvania

Capstone
press

Mankato, Minnesota

First Facts is published by Capstone Press,
151 Good Counsel Drive, P.O. Box 669, Mankato, Minnesota 56002.
www.capstonepress.com

Library of Congress Cataloging-in-Publication Data
Olien, Rebecca.
   Motion / by Rebecca Olien.
   p. cm.—(First facts. Our physical world)
   Includes bibliographical references and index.
   Contents: Motion—Force—Speed—Friction—Isaac Newton—Action and reaction—Using
motion—Safety in motion—Amazing but true!—Hands on: balloon traveler.
   ISBN-13: 978-0-7368-2618-1 (hardcover)   ISBN-10: 0-7368-2618-1 (hardcover)
   ISBN-13: 978-0-7368-5158-9 (softcover pbk.)   ISBN-10: 0-7368-5158-5 (softcover pbk.)
   1. Motion—Juvenile literature. [1. Motion.] I. Title. II. Series.
QC133.5.O44 2005
531'.11'078—dc22   2003026086

Summary: Introduces motion and provides instructions for an activity to demonstrate
      some of its characteristics.

Editorial Credits
Christopher Harbo, editor; Linda Clavel, series designer; Molly Nei, book designer;
   Scott Thoms, photo researcher; Eric Kudalis, product planning editor

Photo Credits
Capstone Press/Gary Sundermeyer, cover, 6, 8–9, 10–11, 14, 16, 18
Corbis/LWA-Sharie Kennedy, 4–5; Milepost 90½/Colin Garratt, 17; Norbert Schaefer, 19
Digital Vision, 15
©J H Peterson, 7
Seapics.com/Avi Klapfer, 20
Stock Montage Inc., 13

1 2 3 4 5 6 09 08 07 06 05 04

Table of Contents

Motion

Motion happens when something moves from place to place. The earth moves around the sun. People move while working and playing. Animals swim, fly, or walk from place to place. Machine parts move back and forth to do work.

Force

Nothing can move by itself. Things move when a **force** pushes or pulls them. A force changes the motion, **speed**, or direction of something.

Wind has force. The wind pushes
on the sail of a sailboat. The boat then
moves through the water.

Speed

Speed is how fast something moves. Speed is measured by the amount of time something takes to move from place to place. More force makes things move faster. A hard push moves a toy car fast. A light push moves a toy car slowly.

Fun Fact!
The fastest airplane is the SR-71 Blackbird. It can fly up to 2,200 miles (3,500 kilometers) per hour.

Friction

Friction is a force that slows objects down. Rubbing things together makes friction. Bicycle brakes use friction to slow down a bike. Rubber pads rub on the rim of a wheel. The friction between the pads and the rim stops the wheel.

Fun Fact!
Skiers put wax on their skis so there is less friction between the skis and the snow.

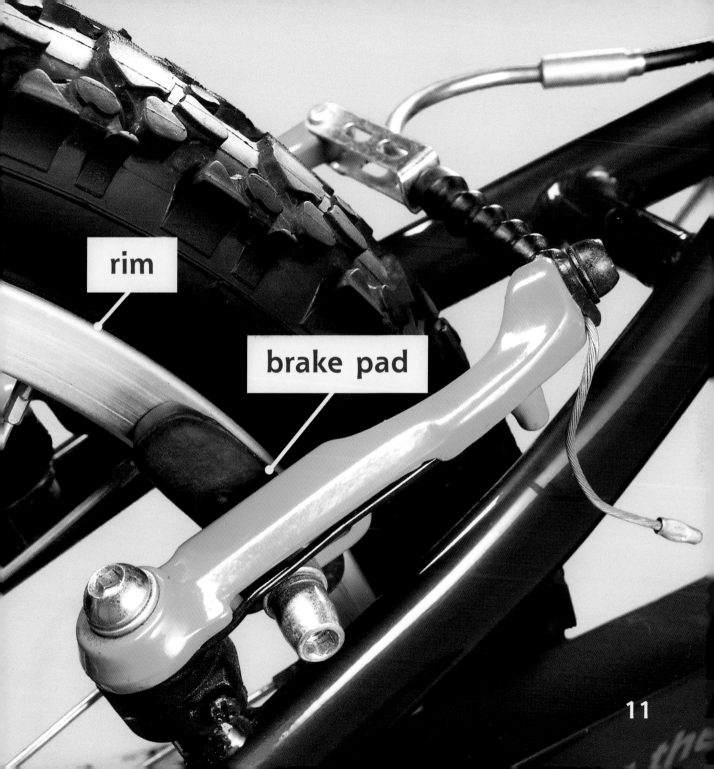

rim

brake pad

Isaac Newton

Isaac Newton was an English scientist in the 1600s. He studied how things move. In 1687, Newton wrote three **laws** about motion. These laws are called Newton's Laws of Motion. His third law is the most famous. It says that every action has an equal and **opposite reaction**.

13

Action and Reaction

Every motion creates an opposite action. People push back with their feet to walk forward. Paddles sweep water back to move a boat forward.

Rockets use action and reaction to fly. Blasts of hot gases push a space shuttle into space.

Fun Fact!
Squids move forward and backward by squirting out jets of water.

Using Motion

People use machines with moving parts to do work. Mixers use motion to blend cake batter.

People also use motion to travel. Trains, cars, and airplanes quickly move people over long distances.

Safety in Motion

Moving fast can be dangerous. A sudden change of speed or direction can cause accidents. People should wear seat belts when riding in a car.

People should protect themselves while playing. They should wear a helmet when in-line skating. Pads also help to protect people from getting hurt.

Amazing but True!

The sailfish is the fastest fish in the ocean. The sailfish can swim up to 60 miles (97 kilometers) per hour. Its sail-like fin and long, thin body help it move fast.

Hands On: Balloon Traveler

A balloon traveler is a fun toy you can make. You can use the balloon traveler to experiment with motion.

What You Need

small balloon
plastic straw
tape

What You Do

1. Place the balloon opening over one end of the straw.
2. Put tape tightly around the straw and balloon opening.
3. Blow into the straw to blow up the balloon.
4. Place a finger over the end of the straw.
5. Lower the straw to a floor without carpet. Keep your finger over the end of the straw.
6. Let go of the straw and watch the balloon traveler move.

Which way does the balloon traveler go? How is the force of air making the straw move? Try sending your balloon traveler over carpet or grass. Does friction change the way the balloon traveler moves?

Glossary

force (FORSS)—something that changes the speed, direction, or motion of an object

friction (FRIK-shuhn)—a force produced when two objects rub against each other; friction slows down objects.

law (LAW)—a statement in science about what always happens when certain events take place

opposite (OP-uh-zit)—facing or moving the other way

reaction (ree-AK-shuhn)—an action in response to something that happens

speed (SPEED)—how fast something moves; speed is a measure of the time it takes something to cover a certain distance.

Read More

Cooper, Christopher. *Forces and Motion: From Push to Shove.* Science Answers. Chicago: Heinemann Library, 2003.

Morgan, Ben. *Motion.* Elementary Physics. San Diego: Blackbirch Press, 2003.

Internet Sites

FactHound offers a safe, fun way to find Internet sites related to this book. All of the sites on FactHound have been researched by our staff.

Here's how:
1. Visit *www.facthound.com*
2. Type in this special code **0736826181** for age-appropriate sites. Or enter a search word related to this book for a more general search.
3. Click on the **Fetch It** button.

FactHound will fetch the best sites for you!

Index